Rutherford

by Iain Gray

Lang**Syne**

PUBLISHING

WRITING *to* REMEMBER

79 Main Street, Newtongrange,
Midlothian EH22 4NA
Tel: 0131 344 0414
E-mail: info@lang-syne.co.uk
www.langsyneshop.co.uk

Design by Dorothy Meikle
Printed by Printwell Ltd
© Lang Syne Publishers Ltd 2024

All rights reserved. No part of this publication may be reproduced, stored or introduced into a retrieval system, or transmitted in any form or by any means (electronic, mechanical, photocopying, recording or otherwise) without the prior written permission of Lang Syne Publishers Ltd.

ISBN 978-1-85217-793-5

Rutherford

MOTTO:
Neither by chance nor fate

CREST:
A martlet

TERRITORY:
Scottish Borders

NAME variations include:
Rudferd
Ruterford
Rutherfoord
Rudforde
Rutherfurd

Chapter one:

The origins of the clan system

by Rennie McOwan

The original Scottish clans of the Highlands and the great families of the Lowlands and Borders were gatherings of families, relatives, allies and neighbours for mutual protection against rivals or invaders.

Scotland experienced invasion from the Vikings, the Romans and English armies from the south. The Norman invasion of what is now England also had an influence on land-holding in Scotland. Some of these invaders stayed on and in time became 'Scottish'.

The word clan derives from the Gaelic language term 'clann', meaning children, and it was first used many centuries ago as communities were formed around tribal lands in glens and mountain fastnesses.

The format of clans changed over the centuries, but at its best the chief and his family held the land on behalf of all, like trustees, and the ordinary clansmen and women believed they had a blood relationship with the founder of their clan.

There were two way duties and obligations. An inadequate chief could be deposed and replaced by someone of greater ability.

Clan people had an immense pride in race. Their relationship with the chief was like adult children to a father and they had a real dignity.

The concept of clanship is very old and a more feudal notion of authority gradually crept in.

Pictland, for instance, was divided into seven principalities ruled by feudal leaders who were the strongest and most charismatic leaders of their particular groups.

By the sixth century the 'British' kingdoms of Strathclyde, Lothian and Celtic Dalriada (Argyll) had emerged and Scotland, as one nation, began to take shape in the time of King Kenneth MacAlpin.

Some chiefs claimed descent from ancient kings which may not have been accurate in every case.

By the twelfth and thirteenth centuries the clans and families were more strongly brought under the central control of Scottish monarchs.

Lands were awarded and administered more and more under royal favour, yet the power of the area clan chiefs was still very great.

The long wars to ensure Scotland's

independence against the expansionist ideas of English monarchs extended the influence of some clans and reduced the lands of others.

Those who supported Scotland's greatest king, Robert the Bruce, were awarded the territories of the families who had opposed his claim to the Scottish throne.

In the Scottish Borders country – the notorious Debatable Lands – the great families built up a ferocious reputation for providing warlike men accustomed to raiding into England and occasionally fighting one another.

Chiefs had the power to dispense justice and to confiscate lands and clan warfare produced a society where martial virtues – courage, hardiness, tenacity – were greatly admired.

Gradually the relationship between the clans and the Crown became strained as Scottish monarchs became more orientated to life in the Lowlands and, on occasion, towards England.

The Highland clans spoke a different language, Gaelic, whereas the language of Lowland Scotland and the court was Scots and in more modern times, English.

Highlanders dressed differently, had different

customs, and their wild mountain land sometimes seemed almost foreign to people living in the Lowlands.

It must be emphasised that Gaelic culture was very rich and story-telling, poetry, piping, the clarsach (harp) and other music all flourished and were greatly respected.

Highland culture was different from other parts of Scotland but it was not inferior or less sophisticated.

Central Government, whether in London or Edinburgh, sometimes saw the Gaelic clans as a challenge to their authority and some sent expeditions into the Highlands and west to crush the power of the Lords of the Isles.

Nevertheless, when the eighteenth century Jacobite Risings came along the cause of the Stuarts was mainly supported by Highland clans.

The word Jacobite comes from the Latin for James – Jacobus. The Jacobites wanted to restore the exiled Stuarts to the throne of Britain.

The monarchies of Scotland and England became one in 1603 when King James VI of Scotland (1st of England) gained the English throne after Queen Elizabeth died.

The Union of Parliaments of Scotland and England, the Treaty of Union, took place in 1707.

Some Highland clans, of course, and Lowland families opposed the Jacobites and supported the incoming Hanoverians.

After the Jacobite cause finally went down at Culloden in 1746 a kind of ethnic cleansing took place. The power of the chiefs was curtailed. Tartan and the pipes were banned in law.

Many emigrated, some because they wanted to, some because they were evicted by force. In addition, many Highlanders left for the cities of the south to seek work.

Many of the clan lands became home to sheep and deer shooting estates.

But the warlike traditions of the clans and the great Lowland and Border families lived on, with their descendants fighting bravely for freedom in two world wars.

Remember the men from whence you came, says the Gaelic proverb, and to that could be added the role of many heroic women.

The spirit of the clan, of having roots, whether Highland or Lowland, means much to thousands of people.

Meanwhile, many families proudly boast the heraldic device known as a Coat of Arms,.

The central motif of the Coat of Arms would originally have been what was sometimes borne on the shield of a warrior to distinguish himself from others on the battlefield.

Clan warfare produced a society where courage and tenacity were greatly admired

Chapter two:

Living on the borderline

Taking their name from the lands in the Scottish Borders in which they settled, the Rutherfords and their namesakes the Rutherfurds feature prominently in the pages of the drama that is Scotland's frequently turbulent history.

There are two accounts as to their origins.

According to one tradition, at some indeterminate time a man by the name of Ruther used his local knowledge to safely guide a king of Scots over a ford in the River Tweed.

This allowed the monarch to proceed with his army and gain a great victory over his enemies the Northumbrians and, as a reward, he granted Ruther some lands. Because of the role the ford had played in his good fortune, Ruther and his lands thereafter became known as 'Rutherford'.

Yet another colourful tradition is that an English army, poised threateningly on the heights above the River Tweed, took the foolhardy decision to abandon their strategic position to attack a smaller Scottish force on the opposite side of the river.

With their defences lowered as they struggled to ford the Tweed, they were cut to pieces and the victorious Scots subsequently named the spot 'Rue (Regret) the Ford – eventually rendered as 'Rutherford'.

But whatever the true origin of the surname, what is known with certainty is that from an early date the Rutherfords were established in the lands of the name near the present day hamlet of Maxton, in Roxburghshire.

In the now redundant form 'Rodyforde', a Robertus de (of) Rodyforde is recorded as witness to a charter in about 1140 while, between 1161 and 1272 a Nichol de Rutherford appears in a number of records.

That the name is frequently featured indicates the Rutherfords enjoyed a degree of respectability and trust – and this is borne out by the fact that in 1398, during the reign of King Robert III, Sir Richard Rutherford served as Scottish ambassador to the English court.

But in many ways this 'respectability' was a veneer, as the Rutherfords also had a reputation as one of the feared Border 'reiving' or raiding clans.

This notoriety came from their time-honoured custom of reiving, or raiding, not only their neighbours' livestock but also that of their counterparts across the border – while the word 'bereaved', for example, indicating to have suffered loss, derives from the original 'reived', meaning loss of property.

A constant thorn in the flesh of both the English and Scottish authorities was the cross-border raiding and pillaging carried out by well-mounted and heavily armed men, the contingent from the Scottish side known and feared as 'moss troopers' or 'freebooters'.

In an attempt to bring order to what was known as the wild 'debateable land' on both sides, King Alexander II of Scotland had in 1237 signed the Treaty of York, which for the first time established the Scottish border with England as a line running from the Solway to the Tweed.

On either side there were three 'marches' or areas of administration, the West, East and Middle Marches, and a warden governed these.

Complaints from either side of the border were dealt with on Truce Days, when the wardens of the different marches would act as arbitrators.

There was also a law known as the Hot Trod, that granted anyone who had their livestock stolen the right to pursue the thieves and recover their property.

The post of March Warden was a powerful and lucrative one, with rival families vying for the position, and the marches became virtually a law unto themselves.

In the Scottish borderlands, the Rutherfords, along with others including the Douglases, Taits, Turnbulls and Youngs held sway in the Middle March.

The Homes and Swintons dominated the East March, while the Armstrongs, Maxwells, Johnstones, Grahams and Beatties were the rulers of the West March.

Wardens from the Middle Marches met at locations including Deadwater, on the North Tyne, while those for the East Marches met at Redden Burn, on the Tweed, just west of Wark.

A record exists from 1398 of an agreement between commissioners for Scotland and England that the men of Nithsdale, Galloway, Crawfordmuir and Annandale should meet the wardens of the West March at the 'Clochmabanstane' for redress.

Also known as the Lochmaben Stone, or the Clochmaben Stone, this granite bulk was situated about a mile southwest of Gretna, on a small rise of ground at the head of the Solway Firth, at Sulwath.

Ironically, wardens were chosen from the families of the very bands of reivers that they were, ostensibly at least, pledged to control – the sons of Sir Richard Rutherford, for example, served as wardens.

One of Sir Richard's sons obtained through marriage the lands of Chatto and Hunthill, but this line of the Rutherfords failed and its lands passed to the Traquair family.

One noted branch of the family was the Rutherfords of Edgerston, whose seat was the castle of the name – now the privately-owned Edgerston House – near Jedburgh.

With the spelling variant 'Rutherfurd', one renowned member of the family was Thomas Rutherfurd, known as The Black Laird of Edgerston, famed for a number of daring exploits against the English including the Raid of the Redeswire.

Also known as the Redeswire Fray or the battle of the Red Swire, it took place at the pass through the Cheviot Hills known as Carter Bar, at Redesdale, in July of 1575.

This was the date on which Sir John Carmichael, Warden of the Middle March, met his English counterpart Sir John Forster, who was accompanied by Sir George Heron, Keeper of Redesdale, for a Truce Day to discuss matters of mutual concern.

By custom in these volatile times, the wardens were guarded by heavily armed men, and tempers flared when Carmichael demanded that a notorious English freebooter known as Farnstein – in Forster's custody – be handed over to face justice for crimes committed on the Scottish side of the border.

But Forster claimed Farnstein had taken what was euphemistically known as 'leg-bail' – escaped from custody – leading to insults being traded by both sides.

Matters came to a head when some of Forster's retinue attacked the Scots, killing two men and wounding a number of others.

It was while beating a disorganised and hasty retreat that the Scots met up with the Black Laird of Edgerston and his battle-hardened moss troopers – who had been delayed en route for the meeting at Redesdale.

Gaining new confidence with the arrival of Rutherfurd and his men, the Scots rallied and routed the English contingent.

Sir John Heron, along with his brother and 23 others were killed while Forster, along with other high ranking Englishmen including Francis Russell, son of the Earl of Bedford, were taken prisoner and confined for ransom in Dalkeith Castle.

To add insult to already grievous injury, the Scots also took the opportunity to help themselves to 300 head of cattle from surrounding English farms.

What had started as a Border skirmish took a much more serious turn when news of the affair reached Queen Elizabeth.

Decidedly not amused, she threatened dire repercussions unless 'immediate satisfaction' was forthcoming.

Wishing to avoid full-scale war with the English queen the Regent Morton, in charge of Scottish affairs, released Forster and his fellow prisoners, offering them profuse apologies and showering them with gifts and also agreeing for Sir John Carmichael to be taken as a prisoner for trial at York.

Surprisingly, the English court acquitted him on the grounds that Forster had committed an unprovoked attack.

The incident which had nearly taken Scotland

and England to war and in which Thomas Rutherfurd, the Black Laird of Edgerston had played a key role, is remembered to this day in the form of the Redeswire Stone, erected in commemoration of the battle and whose inscription reads:

> *On this ridge, June 7, 1575 was fought*
> *one of the last border raids, known as*
> *the Raid of the Redeswire.*

Also keeping the memory fresh is the annual Jedburgh Reidswire Common Riding, involving two horses rode at fast pace.

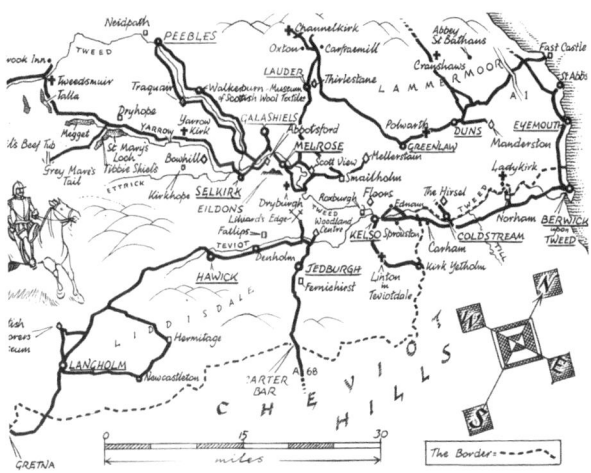

Chapter three:

Honours and distinction

In the seventeenth century, the Rutherford lairds of Edgerston became embroiled in the bitter and bloody wars between Crown and Covenant.

Also known as the British Civil Wars and of which the English Civil War formed a part, they were sparked off in Scotland during the Bishops' Wars of 1639 and 1640.

These had their origin in the widely unpopular attempt by King Charles I to impose uniform religious practice between the Church of England and the proudly independent Scottish Kirk, through the introduction into Scotland of the Episcopal Book of Common Prayer.

Matters came to a head with the signing on February 28, 1638 of the *National Covenant* – a document as important to Scottish history as the equally famed *Declaration of Arbroath* of 1320.

Described as 'the glorious marriage day of the kingdom with God', the Covenant renounced Roman Catholic belief, pledged to uphold the Presbyterian religion and called for free parliaments and assemblies.

First signed at Edinburgh's Greyfriars Kirk by nobles, barons, burgesses and ministers, it was subscribed to the following day by hundreds of common folk.

Copies were made and dispatched around the nation and signed by thousands more – with its adherents becoming known as Covenanters.

This led to a civil war that raged between Covenanters and Royalists.

Rutherford, the laird of Edgerston, raised a troop of horse that fought for the cause of King Charles II at the battle of Dunbar in September of 1650, about a year after Charles I was executed by order of the English Parliament.

The Scottish Covenanting army suffered a crushing defeat at the hands of England's 'Lord Protector' Oliver Cromwell and his New Model Army with some accounts stating there were more than 3,000 killed and up to 10,000 taken prisoner – many later transported as slaves to the colonies.

The laird of Edgerston was severely wounded and most of his men killed.

While he had fought in support of the Crown, the Presbyterian minister the Rev Samuel Rutherford, of the Hunthill branch of the family, was a staunch adherent of the Covenant. Born in about 1600 in what is now the Roxburghshire parish of Crailing, he became a leading theologian after an education that included Jedburgh Academy and the University of Edinburgh.

Minister for the parish of Anworth, in southwest Scotland, and one of the four main Commissioners of the Church of Scotland, he became noted for fearlessly preaching before Charles II at St Andrews in 1650 on the duty of kings.

The monarch never forgave this perceived insult to his royal person and on Restoration in 1660 he ordered that Rutherford's book *Lex Rex –The Law is King* –was publicly burned at St Andrews and Edinburgh by the public hangman.

Deprived of all offices, he died in 1661 shortly after being cited to appear before the Scottish Parliament on a charge of treason.

But his defiant stance in the face of royal power is remembered to this day in the form of a monument erected to his memory in 1842 on a hilltop overlooking what had been his parish of Anworth.

More fortunate in his lifetime than the Rev Samuel Rutherford, Andrew Rutherford acquired high honours and distinction following the Restoration.

Born in Edinburgh, he was the son of a wealthy merchant and civic official and of the Chatto and Hunthill branch of the Rutherfords.

Taking up a military career and serving with a Scottish regiment in the service of King Louis XIV of France, it was on the monarch's recommendation that he was taken into the service of Charles II in 1660.

Created Lord Rutherford a year later and given the governorship of Dunkirk, when the town was subsequently sold by Charles to France he was given command of the Colony of Tangier and the Tangier Regiment and further elevated in the peerage as 1st Earl of Teviot.

Dying in 1664 without a recognised male heir, the earldom of Teviot became extinct, but his estates and titles passed to his cousin Sir Thomas Rutherford of Hunthill.

In the following century and with the popular Rutherford spelling variant 'Rutherfurd', Walter Rutherfurd was the Scots-American soldier and merchant remembered as a founder of what thrives to this day as the Saint Andrew's Society of the State of New York.

Of the Edgerston branch of the family and born there in 1723, the son of Sir John and Elizabeth Rutherfurd (née Cairncross), he held a number of military commands including – in what was then the British colony of America – as a major in the Colonial Army.

Later establishing himself as a prominent New York businessman, by 1771 he was one of its wealthiest citizens.

A founder of the New York Hospital and serving as its governor from 1774 to 1778, in 1756 he had also been a founder of the Saint Andrew's Society of the State of New York, serving as its president from 1766 to 1767 and again from 1792 to 1798.

He died in 1804, while the charity today is the oldest charitable institution in the state.

Dedicated to helping needy Scots or lineal descendants of Scots in the New York community, and with its offices on East 55th Street, Manhattan, among its social events is the annual Tartan Day Parade through the city.

In politics and across the border from the United States, Alexander Rutherford, born in 1857 on a dairy farm in Ormond, in what was then Canada West, was the lawyer and politician who served from 1905 to 1910 as the first premier of Alberta.

The son of Scottish immigrants to Canada, he died in 1941.

Bearers of the Rutherford name have also excelled in the worlds of science and medicine.

A grandfather of the great Scottish novelist and antiquarian Sir Walter Scott, John Rutherford was the pioneering physician born in Edinburgh in 1695.

One of the founding professors of the University of Edinburgh Medical School and a Fellow of the Royal College of Physicians of Edinburgh, he was instrumental in the introduction of what is now the universal practice of medical students receiving clinical teaching not only in the classroom but also through 'hands-on' experience in hospitals.

He died in 1779, while he was the father of the physician, chemist and botanist Daniel Rutherford, born in Edinburgh in 1749.

Known for the isolation of the gas nitrogen in 1772, a joint founder of the Royal Society of Edinburgh, professor of botany at the University of Edinburgh and president of the Royal College of Physicians of Edinburgh from 1796 to 1798, he died in 1819.

Known as the father of nuclear physics, Ernest Rutherford was the son of a Scottish father and English mother who had immigrated to New Zealand before his birth in 1871. Born in Brightwater, near Nelson, his father was a farmer and his mother a teacher, and Rutherford rose to become one of the greatest experimental physicists of his age.

Among his first discoveries were the concept of radioactive half-life, the radioactive element radon and the difference between alpha and beta radiation.

This was while carrying out work at McGill University, Montreal, and which led to him receiving the 1908 Nobel Prize in Chemistry.

Having moved a year before this to the Victoria University of Manchester, now the University of Manchester, he carried out the first artificial nuclear reaction by bombarding nitrogen nuclei with alpha particles.

This resulted in the emission of sub-atomic particles that he later named protons, while it was under his direction as director of the Cavendish Laboratory at the University of Cambridge in 1932 that James Chadwick discovered the neutron.

Also under his direction and in the same year, John Cockcroft and Ernest Walton carried out the first experiment to split the nucleus of an atom in a fully controlled manner.

Raised to the peerage in 1931 as 1st Baron

Rutherford of Nelson and with a host of other honours and awards including an inaugural recipient of the Royal Society of New Zealand's T.K. Sidey Medal for outstanding scientific research, he died in 1937.

He also received the high honour of being interred in Westminster Abbey – very fittingly near Isaac Newton and other great scientific luminaries, while in 1997 the chemical element rutherfordium (element 104) was named after him.

Sir Ernest Rutherford, the father of nuclear physics

Chapter four:

On the world stage

Born in 1892 in Balham, South London, Margaret Taylor Benn was the award-winning English actress of stage, television and film better known as Margaret Rutherford and more formally as Dame Margaret Rutherford.

Her childhood was beset by family tragedies that had their source long before her birth when her father William Rutherford Benn, after suffering a nervous breakdown and confined for a time in Bethnal House Lunatic Asylum, murdered his father the Rev Julius Benn in 1883 by bludgeoning him to death with a chamber pot.

Slashing his own throat with a pocketknife before being apprehended, he was declared insane and sent to Broadmoor Lunatic Asylum.

Discharged in 1890 and reunited with his wife Florence, he subsequently legally dropped 'Benn' from his surname before later seeking a fresh start in life with his family in Madras, India.

Margaret, their only child, accompanied her parents to India – but tragedy struck again when her pregnant mother took her own life after hanging herself from a tree outside the family home

Aged only three, she returned to Britain to be raised by an aunt who left her a small legacy on her death that allowed her to study acting.

But it was not until 1925, when aged 33, that she made her stage debut after having worked for a time as a piano and elocution teacher.

First coming to the attention of critics in 1939 in a production of Oscar Wilde's *The Importance of Being Earnest*, acclaim came two years later in the role of Madame Arcati in Noel Coward's *Blithe Spirit* – with the critic Kenneth Tynan remarking: "The unique thing about Margaret Rutherford is that she can act with her chin alone."

Her screen debut followed four years later in a film adaptation of *Blithe Spirit*, with further success through comedic roles in other films – culminating in both an Academy award and Golden Globe Award for her role of the Duchess of Brighton in the 1963 *The V.I.P.s*.

Other major credits include the 1949 *Passport to Pimlico*, the 1957 *The Smallest Show on Earth* and, from 1959, *I'm All Right Jack*, while also starring in the memorable role of Miss Jane Marple in a series of films based on the novels of Agatha Christie.

In 1945, meanwhile, she had married the character actor Stringer Davis who devotedly cared for her through periodic bouts of debilitating depression – for which she occasionally received electric shock treatment.

Appointed an OBE in 1961 and a Dame six years later, the much-loved actress from such a tragic background died in 1972 – while one genealogical footnote is that through her father's side of the family she was related to the British Labour Party politician Tony Benn.

Known for her role of Carreen O'Hara, a sister of Scarlett O'Hara in the 1939 film *Gone with the Wind* and of Polly Benedict in the *Andy Hardy* youth comedy film series, **Ann Rutherford** was the Canadian-American actress of radio, film and television born in 1917 in Vancouver, British Columbia.

With other screen credits including a number of Westerns co-starring with John Wayne and Gene Autry, the 1940 *Pride and Prejudice*, the 1943 *Whistling in Brooklyn* and, three years before her retirement from the stage in 1950, *The Secret Life of Walter Mitty*, she died in 2012.

Bearers of the Rutherford name have also excelled in the highly competitive world of sport.

Born in 1986 in Bletchley, Milton Keynes, **Greg Rutherford** is the British retired track and field athlete who specialised in the long jump.

Winner of the gold medal at the 2012 Olympics, 2014 Commonwealth Games, 2014 and 2016 European Athletic Championships and top of the rankings at the 2015 IAAF (International Amateur Athletics Federation) Diamond League Championships, at the time of writing he holds the British record in long jump for both outdoors and indoors.

The recipient of the 2018 European Athletics Lifetime Achievement Award and an MBE for services to athletics, in 2019 he won the BBC's *Celebrity MasterChef* competition.

On the football pitch his grandfather **John Rutherford**, born in 1907 and who died in 1983 and his great-grandfather **Jock Rutherford**, born in 1884 and who died in 1963, were both noted Arsenal players.

Also in football, **William Rutherford**, born in 1945 in Lochgelly, Fife was the Scottish player who immigrated to Australia in 1969 after playing for teams including East Fife.

Having played for Sydney Hakoah, represented the state of New South Wales and earning three caps with the Australia national team, he died in 2010.

On the cricket pitch, **Ken Rutherford**, born in Dunedin in 1965, is the New Zealand former player who captained his national team for a period during the 1990s.

A Member of the New Zealand Order of Merit for services to the sport, he is the father of the cricketer **Hamish Rutherford**, born in 1989 and who has also represented his country – as has his uncle **Ian Rutherford**, born in 1957.

Back on British shores and in rugby union, **John Rutherford**, also known as 'Rud' or 'Ruddie', is the Scottish former fly-half who, in addition to playing for clubs including Selkirk R.F.C. and South of Scotland, earned 42 caps playing for his nation between 1979 and 1987.

Still on the rugby pitch, **Donald Rutherford**, born in 1937, is the England former international rugby union player who played for teams including RAF and Combined Services, Wasps, Northumberland and Gloucester.

Appointed in 1969 the first technical director

of the Rugby Football Union at Twickenham and instrumental in a number of important playing and coaching initiatives, he was the recipient of an OBE for services to the game in 2000.

From sport to the creative world of the written word and with the Rutherford spelling variant 'Rutherfurd', **Edward Rutherfurd** is the pen-name of the best-selling historical British novelist Francis Edward Wintle.

Born in 1948 in Salisbury, Wiltshire, he abandoned a career in political research, bookselling and publishing to write *Sarum* – an epic tale spanning a 10,000-year period – and centred on his home town and the nearby mysterious megalith of Stonehenge.

Published in 1987 and remaining on the New York Times Bestseller List for 23 weeks, it has been followed by other books including *New York: The Novel*, winner of awards including the 2009 Langum Prize for American Historical Fiction.

In the equally creative world of music, **James Rutherford** is the internationally acclaimed British bass-baritone opera singer born in 1972 in Norwich.

Having studied singing at the Royal College of Music, London and the National Opera Studio, his stage debut came in 1999 singing the title role of Verdi's Falstaff, while in 2006 he won the Seattle Opera International Wagner Competition.

A regular performer with the Graz Opera of Austria, including as Wotan in *Der Ring des Nibelungen*, his best-selling solo recordings include the 2014 *Rutherford Sings Wagner*.

In a decidedly different music genre, Michael John Cloete Crawford Rutherford is the English singer, songwriter and guitarist better known as **Mike Rutherford**, a co-founder of the progressive rock band Genesis.

Receiving his first guitar when aged eight, it was while a pupil at the exclusive Charterhouse Public School in Godalming, Surrey, that in 1967 he formed Genesis along with fellow pupils Peter Gabriel, Chris Stewart and Tony Banks – to be joined later by the non-privately educated Phil Collins as drummer.

The band enjoyed great success with hits that include *Follow You Follow Me*, *Turn It On Again*, *Throwing It All Away* and *Land of Confusion*, while Rutherford has also gained recognition through his band Mike and the Mechanics, first formed in 1985 – while it was as a member of his first band that he was inducted into the Rock and Roll Hall of Fame in 2010.